GO SAILING!

A practical handbook
for young people

Foreword   By Dame Ellen MacArthur

Chapter One
Where Do I Start?   5

   Just add water   7
   What is a dinghy?   8
   Where do I learn?   9
   What gear do I need?   11

Chapter Two
How Do I Learn the Ropes?   13

   Sailing has its own language   15
   When is a rope not a rope?   16
   More about sails   17
   Getting ready to launch   18
   Into the water   19
   Sailing from a mooring
   or pontoon   20

Chapter Three
How Does It All Work?   21

   How to steer the boat   23
   Look at wind in a new way   24
   Tacking   26
   Reaching up and down   27
   Using the centreboard /
   daggerboard   28
   How to balance the boat   29
   Boat trim and the
   five principles   30
   Gybing   31
   Lookout!   32

Chapter Four
How Do I Slow Down and Stop?   33

   Keeping control   35
   Approaching shore   36
   How to pick up a mooring   38

Chapter Five
How Do I Choose A Boat?   39

   How much will it cost?   41
   Where can I keep her?   42
   What type do I choose?   43
   Where do I launch?   46

Chapter Six
How Do I Stay Safe?   47

   Avoid that sinking feeling   49
   How to avoid collisions   50
   What if I capsize?   52
   How to make a tow   53
   Man Overboard!   54
   What if the wind drops?   55
   Independent sailing   56
   How to call for help   56

Chapter Seven
What Else Do I Need To Know?   57

   Weather basics   59
   What about wind direction?   60
   How do we measure wind strength?   61
   What about tides?   62
   Tidal flow   63
   How do you stop in tidal waters?   64
   Get knotted!   66
   Look after your boat...   67

Chapter Eight
What Next?   69

   Sailing faster   71
   Start racing!   72
   Lets go exploring!   74
   Go sailing!   76

Glossary   78

Useful Websites   84

Foreword

I have been sailing since I can remember, from the first time I went out on the water I loved every minute of it, there is no feeling like it on earth. I hope that this book will help you to understand sailing a little better and perhaps one day soon B&Q and I will see you out on the water! I hope that you get as much enjoyment from reading this book as I have, I wish you good luck for the future and just go for it!

Ellen MacArthur
Skipper Trimaran B&Q
www.teamellen.com

Written and Illustrated by Claudia Myatt

Editors   Sally Kilpatrick
                               David Ritchie

Index   James Pidduck

Layout   Creative Byte

Printed through   World Print

Thanks to:

Laser UK, Topper, RS Sailboats, Lucy at Offshore
Challenges, James Crickmere and all his sailing
friends.

Published by
The Royal Yachting Association
RYA House Ensign Way Hamble
Southampton SO31 4YA
Tel: 0845 345 0400
Fax: 0845 345 0329
Email: info@rya.org.uk
Web: www.rya.org.uk

WHERE DO I START?

7   JUST ADD WATER!

8   WHAT IS A DINGHY?

9   WHERE DO I LEARN?

11   WHAT GEAR DO I NEED?

Anyone can learn to sail; it's easier now than ever before. You don't need to have your own boat to start with, in fact it's better not to rush out and buy one straight away as sailing with other people is the best way to begin. Here's where it all starts......

JUST ADD WATER! Before you rush out and buy a boat, have a think about what sort of sailing you want to do. Sailing means different things to different people, so what do you fancy.....?

WHAT IS A DINGHY? A dinghy is where a lot of sailors begin, a small sailing boat available in all sorts of shapes and sizes. There are over 100 types to choose from, depending on what kind of sailing you want to do. Here are a few basic types:

SINGLE HANDED

"... and the intrepid single handed sailor sets off on his record breaking solo voyage around the lake.... "

... OR A BOAT FOR TWO

"...I'm not pulling any more of your silly ropes unless you say 'please'.'..

A BOAT FOR RACING .....

"... I told you to go to the toilet before you left the clubhouse!"

.... OR FAMILY SAILING

"Well, if Uncle George holds the ice creams , perhaps Grandma could pull in the jib sheet ...."

Some boats strike a balance between cruising and racing so you can enjoy both.

There's more about different types of boat in chapter 5, which helps you choose one to buy, but to begin with you'll be sailing in other people's boats.... the next few pages tell you how.

WHERE DO I LEARN? If you've never sailed before and want to learn, there are several ways to get out on the water safely

JOIN A SAILING CLUB WHICH HAS A JUNIOR SECTION If you don't live near the coast, look for a lake or reservoir inland that does sailing. The Royal Yachting Association is the governing body of sailing and has a website with a list of UK clubs www.rya.org.uk

SAILING CLUBS have lots of useful things......

...CLUBHOUSE WITH BAR —helps keep parents occupied and usually cooks good chips

...RESCUE BOATS

...LOTS OF FRIENDS TO SAIL WITH

SLIPWAY FOR LAUNCHING

...YOU CAN TRY DIFFERENT TYPES OF BOAT TO HELP YOU DECIDE WHAT TO BUY

SPACE TO KEEP TRAILERS AND BOATS

MUDDY BOTTOM SAILING CLUB

Most clubs concentrate on racing, but even if you are not interested in competitive sailing, club races are a useful training ground. You need to be able to sail your boat as well as you can if you want to go off exploring safely on your own.

Chapter One

GO TO A SAILING SCHOOL. RYA recognised training centres run a Youth Sailing Scheme. This starts with 'A taste of sailing' and can take you all the way to advanced techniques and racing if you want to go that far. If you can persuade your family to go on holiday to a place with a sailing school, you can learn somewhere warm! There are RYA schools on the Mediterranean and Caribbean.

GET SOMEONE EXPERIENCED TO TAKE YOU AS CREW Make sure you are properly kitted out for the water - the next page will tell you how.

WHAT GEAR DO I NEED? When you start sailing, you don't need to buy a lot of expensive kit straightaway. You can often borrow buoyancy aids, lifejackets, wetsuits or waterproofs from a sailing school or club. Clubs are also a good place to pick up second hand gear. The main things are to keep SAFE, keep WARM and, if possible, keep DRY!

LIFEJACKETS AND BUOYANCY AIDS

READY?

If there are leg straps, make sure you use them

Whenever you are on or near the water it is vital to wear a lifejacket or buoyancy aid.

What's the difference? A buoyancy aid helps a conscious person to stay afloat. This is usually the most appropriate choice for a dinghy as long as you are water confident.

A lifejacket will support an unconscious person with their face clear of the water.

If you borrow a buoyancy aid or lifejacket, make sure it fits properly!

KEEPING WARM

Keeping warm is very important. It is nearly always cooler on the water than on shore, so don't get caught out. Take spare layers with you if you can.

Modern fleeces and thermals are lightweight as well as warm - avoid clothes that are bulky and heavy!

The key to staying warm is, of course, staying dry, or staying warm when wet! More about this over the page.

READY?

BAD IDEA

Wellies are not a good idea on a dinghy - if you capsize they can fill with water and pull you down.

STAYING DRY - Yes, you will get wet! You need the right gear if you want to avoid getting cold and fed up. How you do this depends on what kind of boat you're sailing.

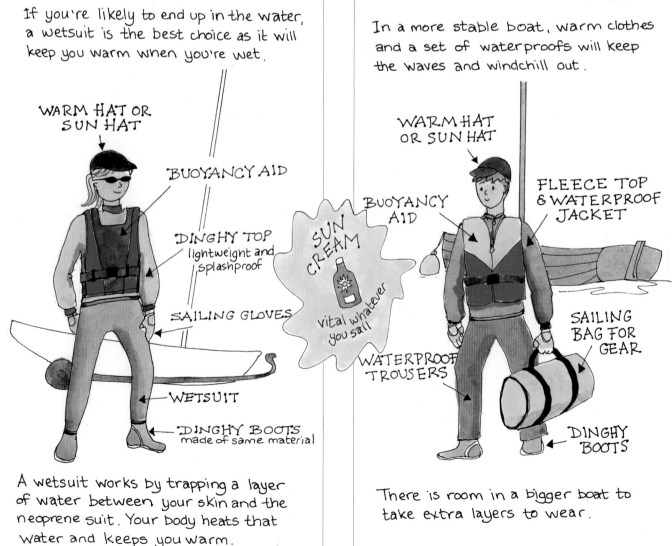

If you're likely to end up in the water, a wetsuit is the best choice as it will keep you warm when you're wet.

WARM HAT OR SUN HAT

BUOYANCY AID

DINGHY TOP
lightweight and splashproof

SAILING GLOVES

WETSUIT

DINGHY BOOTS
made of same material

A wetsuit works by trapping a layer of water between your skin and the neoprene suit. Your body heats that water and keeps you warm.

In a more stable boat, warm clothes and a set of waterproofs will keep the waves and windchill out.

WARM HAT OR SUN HAT

BUOYANCY AID

FLEECE TOP & WATERPROOF JACKET

SUN CREAM
vital whatever you sail

WATERPROOF TROUSERS

SAILING BAG FOR GEAR

DINGHY BOOTS

There is room in a bigger boat to take extra layers to wear.

HOW DO I LEARN THE ROPES?

15 SAILING HAS ITS OWN LANGUAGE

16 WHEN IS A ROPE NOT A ROPE?

17 MORE ABOUT SAILS

18 GETTING READY TO LAUNCH

19 INTO THE WATER

20 SAILING FROM A MOORING OR PONTOON

The language of sailing can seem very confusing to a beginner, but boats are a lot simpler now than they used to be! This chapter looks at what bits of a boat are called and how they all fit together.

SAILING HAS ITS OWN LANGUAGE - this is not just to confuse landlubbers but an essential part of sailing. Here are a few basic words to start with:

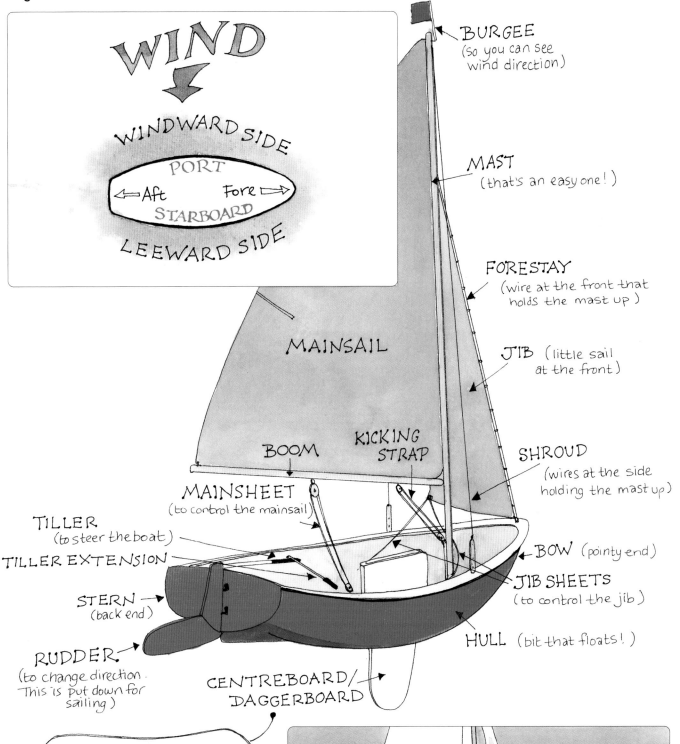

WIND

WINDWARD SIDE
PORT
←Aft   Fore →
STARBOARD
LEEWARD SIDE

BURGEE
(so you can see wind direction)

MAST
(that's an easy one!)

FORESTAY
(wire at the front that holds the mast up)

JIB (little sail at the front)

MAINSAIL

KICKING STRAP

BOOM

SHROUD
(wires at the side holding the mast up)

MAINSHEET
(to control the mainsail)

TILLER
(to steer the boat)

TILLER EXTENSION

BOW (pointy end)

JIB SHEETS
(to control the jib)

STERN
(back end)

HULL (bit that floats!)

RUDDER
(to change direction. This is put down for sailing)

CENTREBOARD/ DAGGERBOARD

What's the difference?
A daggerboard can be moved up or down and taken out completely. Common in singlehanders.

A centreboard is fixed into the boat and pivots forward and backwards.

"PULL IN THE RED ROPE AND WEDGE IT INTO THE PLASTIC CLIP THINGUMMY...."

Chapter Two

WHEN IS A ROPE NOT A ROPE? When it's on a boat! Every rope on board has a name connected to its function. These are the most important ones.....

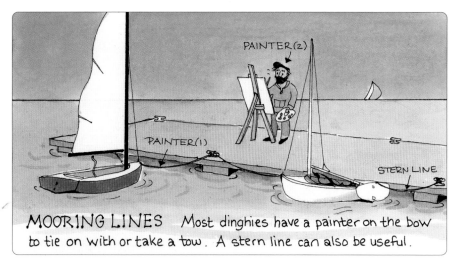

PAINTER (2)

PAINTER (1)

STERN LINE

MOORING LINES
Most dinghies have a painter on the bow to tie on with or take a tow. A stern line can also be useful.

HALYARDS
These are for hoisting sails. The jib halyard hoists the jib and the main halyard hoists the mainsail.

PULL ROPE DOWN

SAIL GOES UP

SHEETS
These ropes control the sails. The mainsail has one sheet ....

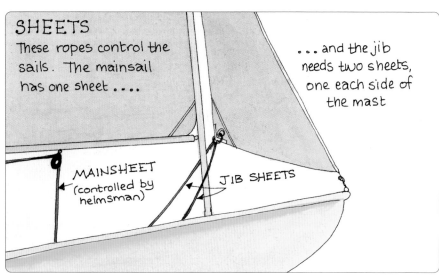

... and the jib needs two sheets, one each side of the mast

MAINSHEET (controlled by helmsman)

JIB SHEETS

HOW ROPES ARE HELD IN PLACE.....
These are CLEATS which hold the ropes so you don't have to.

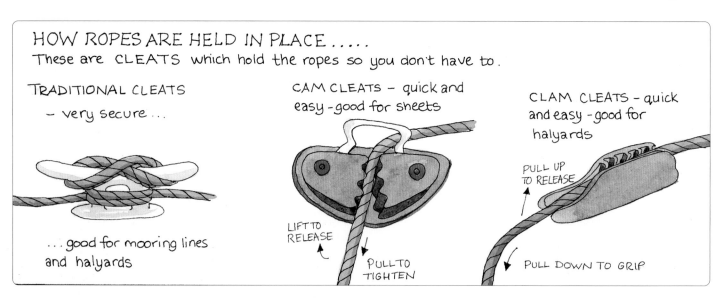

TRADITIONAL CLEATS
– very secure ...

... good for mooring lines and halyards

CAM CLEATS – quick and easy – good for sheets

LIFT TO RELEASE

PULL TO TIGHTEN

CLAM CLEATS – quick and easy – good for halyards

PULL UP TO RELEASE

PULL DOWN TO GRIP

There are lots of other ropes on board – some boats are more complicated than others. Don't get your head too tangled up with them all just yet.......

MORE ABOUT SAILS. Most dinghy sails are triangular. You need to learn the names of each part of the sail.

The combination of the sails and mast together make a rig. Different boats have different rigs - you don't have to learn all these names yet (unless you want to impress your family) but here's a few to look out for....

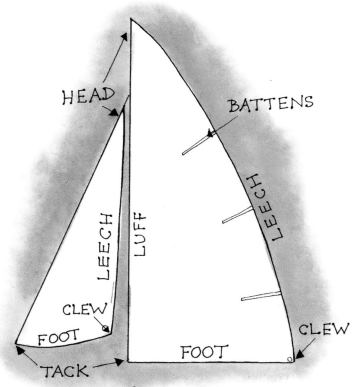

HEAD

BATTENS

LEECH

LUFF

LEECH

CLEW

FOOT

CLEW

FOOT

TACK

BERMUDAN RIG
The most common rig, found on most modern dinghies

GUNTER RIG
Two spars instead of one tall mast means it's easy to car-top.

SPRIT RIG
A short mast, ideal for children

LUG RIG
Again, part of the sail is hoisted on a separate spar. A jib can be added.

GAFF RIG
A traditional rig found on some larger dinghies.

I JUST HAVEN'T GOT A CLEW....

GETTING READY TO LAUNCH is called RIGGING, and most of this can be done ashore while the boat is on its trolley. The most important thing is to make sure the boat is facing into the wind before putting any sails up.

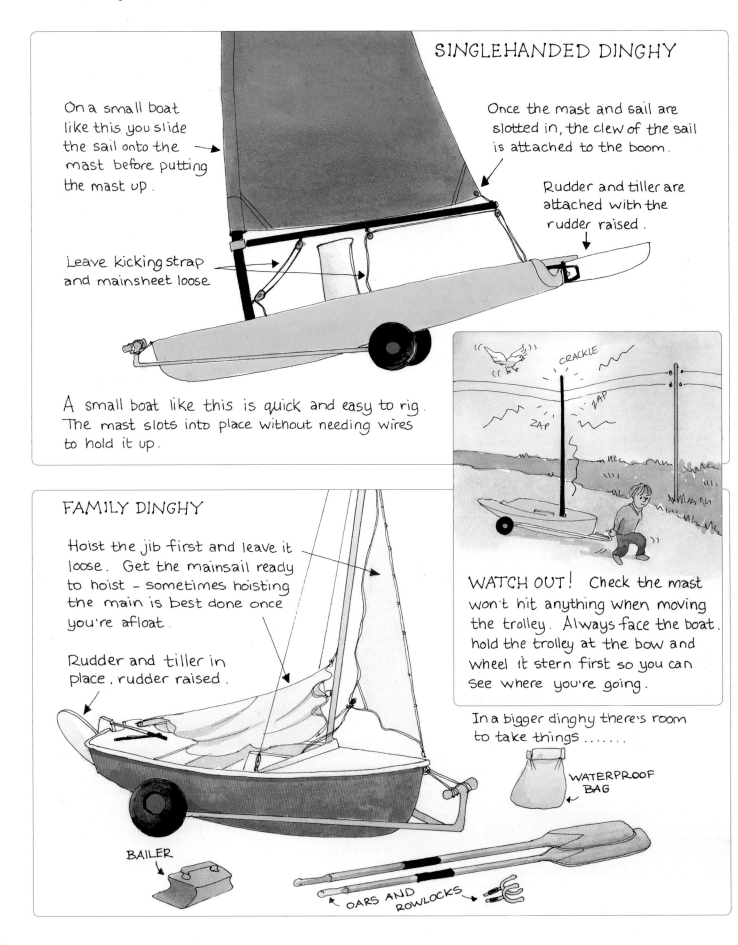

SINGLEHANDED DINGHY

On a small boat like this you slide the sail onto the mast before putting the mast up.

Once the mast and sail are slotted in, the clew of the sail is attached to the boom.

Rudder and tiller are attached with the rudder raised.

Leave kicking strap and mainsheet loose

A small boat like this is quick and easy to rig. The mast slots into place without needing wires to hold it up.

CRACKLE

ZAP

ZAP

FAMILY DINGHY

Hoist the jib first and leave it loose. Get the mainsail ready to hoist - sometimes hoisting the main is best done once you're afloat.

Rudder and tiller in place, rudder raised.

WATCH OUT! Check the mast won't hit anything when moving the trolley. Always face the boat, hold the trolley at the bow and wheel it stern first so you can see where you're going.

In a bigger dinghy there's room to take things ....

WATERPROOF BAG

BAILER

OARS AND ROWLOCKS

INTO THE WATER. Rigged and ready to go? Stop and think about the wind first – which way is it blowing? Look at flags or sails to help you work it out. Wind awareness is as important to a sailor as his boat. For launching, you need to know whether the wind is blowing onto the land from the water (onshore wind) or blowing off the land towards the water (offshore wind), as the technique is different for each. Chapter Seven tells you more about wind and about onshore and offshore winds.

Go slowly and carefully down the slipway, especially if there's weed or mud!

SO THAT'S WHY IT'S CALLED A SLIPWAY!

FREE SPIRIT

LAUNCHING IN AN OFFSHORE WIND

WIND

Launch the boat stern first with both sails hoisted. Float her off the trolley, hold the bow into the wind and put the trolley away. Walk the boat out until you can put a bit of centreboard and rudder down.

When you're ready, push the bow away from the shore, get on board, sheet in the jib and sail away!

LAUNCHING IN AN ONSHORE WIND
Hoist the jib only and launch as before. Then turn the boat round, holding the bow until it is pointing into the wind.

Hoist the mainsail and sail off on a close reach – you'll find out how to do this in the next chapter.

WIND

SAILING FROM A MOORING OR PONTOON. If your boat is already afloat, that makes life easier, doesn't it? At least you can step on board without getting your feet wet. Well, you can if you're careful....

Small boats are very sensitive to weight, so be careful how you step on board . . . . .

> I'M OFF FOR A SAIL, SEE YOU..

.... Never step onto the gunwale (pronounced 'gunnel') - the side of the boat. Step carefully into the middle.

> ...LATER!

Make sure the boat is tied close to the pontoon or that someone is holding it close in for you...

> WON'T MAKE THAT MISTAKE AGAIN!

...If the mooring lines are slack, you'll end up with more than wet feet!

TWANG!

SETTING SAIL FROM A PONTOON

If you have a choice, set off from the downwind side of a pontoon. You'll be able to set your sails as you're head to wind, and the wind will help to push you off.

WIND

On this side you're pinned to the pontoon - tricky!

On this side all you have to do is push the bow off and sail away.

IF YOU ARE IN A TIDAL AREA AND THE TIDE IS FLOWING OPPOSITE TO THE WIND, IT WILL MAKE A DIFFERENCE — MORE ON TIDES IN CHAPTER SEVEN

HOW DOES IT ALL WORK?

23   HOW TO STEER THE BOAT

24   LOOK AT WIND IN A NEW WAY

26   TACKING

27   REACHING UP AND DOWN

28   USING THE CENTREBOARD/DAGGERBOARD

29   HOW TO BALANCE THE BOAT

30   BOAT TRIM AND THE FIVE PRINCIPLES

31   GYBING

32   LOOKOUT!

Whether you want to sail on a pond or cross an ocean, it all begins with sailing theory. When you first go out on the water, it can seem very confusing as there is so much to think about. This chapter will help make sense of it all....

How does it all work?

HOW TO STEER THE BOAT. Steering the boat is called helming and the person doing this is called the HELM or HELMSMAN (yes, even when it's a girl). You steer by easing the tiller away or pulling it towards you. It takes a bit of getting used to as the boat turns in the opposite direction to the way you move the tiller. Here's how it works.....

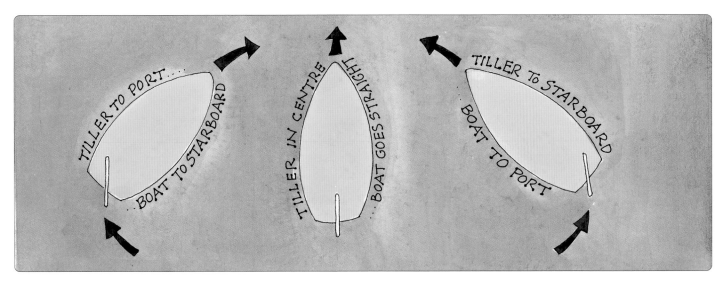

WHERE TO SIT

The helm sits on the windward side of the boat opposite the sail with the tiller or tiller extension in the hand nearest the stern and the mainsheet in the other hand.

Most dinghies have a tiller extension to make helming easier. How you hold this depends on how your boat's mainsheet is set up — either from a block in the centre of the boat (centre main) or from a block at the stern (aft main).

Work out whether you're sailing an aft or centre main boat and hold the tiller extension like this........

WIND

LOOK AT WIND IN A NEW WAY. Wind is the invisible free fuel that makes sailing so exciting. Using it to get your boat where you want to go is very satisfying. Start to develop wind awareness - work out where the wind is coming from in relation to you and your boat. Eventually this will become instinctive. Don't forget the wind can change direction!

These pages show you the POINTS OF SAILING which refer to the boat's course in relation to the wind. They've all got names which you'll need to learn.

CLOSE HAULED. This is as close to the wind as you can go. The sails need to be pulled in tight.

CLOSE REACH. This is not quite so tricky. Let the sails out a little bit.

BEAM REACH. This is the fastest and easiest point of sailing, with the wind on the side of the boat. Let the sails out half way.

BROAD REACH. This takes you a bit further downwind, so let your sails out a bit more.

TRAINING RUN. This keeps the wind slightly to one side of the stern which is easier to steer than a dead run.

RUN. This brings the wind behind you, so the sails could be either side and all the way out.

It can sometimes help to imagine you are sailing in the middle of a cake with a slice missing. The missing piece is always facing the wind and that's the bit you can't sail into . . . .

I TOLD YOU SAILING WAS A PIECE OF CAKE . . . . . .

WIND

WIND STRENGTH
is as important as wind direction. If there's too much wind - or not enough - you could be in trouble. Experienced sailors can cope with more wind than beginners. There's more about wind and weather forecasts in Chapter Seven.

HE..E..E..LP!

WIND

WIND

NO GO ZONE.
(bit you can't sail in)

sails will flap...

...and the boat stops!

SAILING UPWIND. Boats can sail in any direction EXCEPT INTO THE WIND. So if that's the way you want to go you have to zigzag from side to side of the no go zone. This is called beating to windward and involves tacking the boat through about 90 degrees from close hauled to close hauled through the no go zone.

SAIL TRIM. Every time you change direction, even a little bit, you have to adjust the set of the sails. This is done either by 'sheeting in' when turning closer to the wind or 'easing the sheets' when turning away from the wind.

How do you know how far to trim the sails? The simplest way is to pull them in until the sail just stops flapping.

A run is the trickiest to steer as it can be quite unstable. Setting one sail on each side is called goose-winged.

PORT OR STARBOARD TACK?

wind coming over the port side of the boat

PORT TACK

WIND

STARBOARD TACK

wind coming over the starboard side of the boat

Now look at the main diagram again - can you work out which boats are on port tack and which are on starboard tack?

DOG & DUCK

hic!

I'M TACKING, OFFICER!

WIND AWARENESS ....
is something you can practise on shore. Work out where the wind is coming from and where your no-go zone would be.

Just don't go tacking down the High Street!

Chapter Three

TACKING or GOING ABOUT is changing direction by turning the bow of the boat through the wind. Whether the dinghy is centre or aft mainsheet rigged, the process is the same. Let's look at the basics...

TILLER EXTENSION COMES ROUND TO OTHER SIDE

PUSH

STRAIGHTEN UP.

LEE-OH!

READY ABOUT!

HEAD TO WIND

WIND

WIND

WIND

Check area is clear. Helm calls 'Ready about' to warn crew. Crew checks area, uncleats jib and replies 'ready'. If it's aft main, helm changes hands (tiller and main sheet). Helm calls Lee-oh and starts the turn by easing the tiller away towards the sail.

As the boom nears the centreline, helm moves across the boat, facing forward in a centre main boat, aft in an aft main boat. Crew takes the new jib sheet and swaps sides. Helm rotates the tiller extension round the end of the tiller.

As the boom reaches the new side, helm sits down and centralises the tiller as the boat points towards its new target and the mainsail fills. In a centre main boat, the tiller is centralised behind the helm's back while he swaps hands (see Tricky Bits on next page)

WATCH OUT FOR YOUR HEAD ON THE BOOM!

MAKE SURE YOU HAVE ENOUGH SPEED TO COMPLETE THE TACK

CENTRE-BOARD SHOULD BE DOWN

TRICKY BITS .... things that bother beginners about tacking!

① If the boat goes head to wind and stays there ....

This is called 'getting into irons'

To get going again, push the tiller away and push the boom away from you..

PUSH   PUSH

Then pull the tiller towards you, pull in the mainsheet...

PULL   PULL

... and off you go!

... you were probably not going fast enough to complete the turn.

.... this makes the boat go backwards and turn away from the wind.

OR .... another way to get out of irons is to ease the sail and raise the centreboard; wait for the boat to turn away from the wind. Then sail off!

② You've tacked - but now your hands are the wrong way round! Here's what to do ....

centre main

back hand holds tiller extension and mainsheet

So front hand can let go of the tiller and take the sheet

You end up with the tiller behind your back in your front hand and the mainsheet in your back hand....

.... so how do you swap them? Bring the hand holding the sheet across your body to hold tiller and sheet together...

.... now the front hand can take the mainsheet while the back hand brings the tiller extension under your arm to the front.

REACHING UP AND DOWN.... Now you've learnt how to turn round, the easiest course to begin with is sailing across the wind (this is called 'Reaching') in a figure of eight course, tacking at each end. Remember to turn into the wind each time, easing the tiller away from you towards the sail.

W I N D

LEE-OH!   LEE-OH!

READY ABOUT!   READY ABOUT!

Keep the wind on the back of your neck between each turn. Centreboard down.

Chapter Three

HOW TO USE THE CENTREBOARD or DAGGERBOARD. As well as steering the boat and trimming the sails, a sailor has to raise and lower the centreboard or daggerboard to make the boat sail as efficiently as possible. The position of the centreboard/daggerboard is adjusted according to the amount of sideways force on the boat, which is strongest when the boat is close hauled but virtually nothing at all on a run. Here's how it works....

HOW A SAIL WORKS...a bit of science!

Because of the curve of the sail, air flowing round the outside of the sail moves faster than the air on the inside of the sail......

fast air on leeward side

slower air on windward side

TOTAL FORCE

This causes a pressure difference each side of the sail which sucks the sail to leeward. The force created is sideways on to the boom - so when close-hauled the whole boat is pushed sideways. This is where the centreboard or daggerboard comes in.......

LEEWAY

Slipping sideways is called MAKING LEEWAY. Even with the board down you will still make some leeway sailing on a reach or close hauled.

WIND

Look at the wake behind you to see how much leeway you're making.

LEEWAY LIL

steering over here

.....but ending up over here

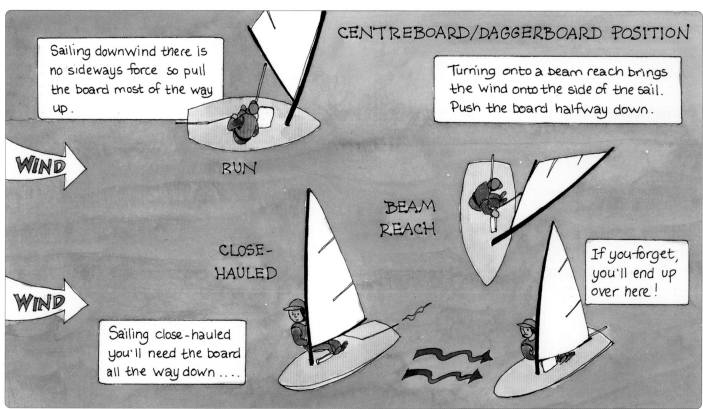

CENTREBOARD/DAGGERBOARD POSITION

Sailing downwind there is no sideways force so pull the board most of the way up.

Turning onto a beam reach brings the wind onto the side of the sail. Push the board halfway down.

WIND

RUN

WIND

BEAM REACH

CLOSE-HAULED

If you forget, you'll end up over here!

Sailing close-hauled you'll need the board all the way down....

HOW TO BALANCE THE BOAT. Boats sail fastest when upright and flat. With the centreboard/daggerboard down resisting the sideways force created by the wind and sails, the boat will heel over. This can be a bit scary for beginners but it's quite normal. The trick is to use your weight to balance the boat and stop her tipping too far - the further out you sit, the more effective your weight will be.

Balancing the boat is important on every point of sailing. On a run, this might mean sitting on opposite sides.

Sailing upwind there is more sideways force and the boat will heel in strong winds. You have to respond quickly to balance the boat. Some have toe straps to help you lean out further.

If the wind is too strong and the boat heeling too much, ease the main sheet a bit. This will take some of the power out of the sail and avoid a capsize.

Heavier dinghies will be less tippy than lightweight boats. But whatever you sail, you'll still need to keep it balanced!

BOAT TRIM. As well as balancing the boat to keep it upright, you also need to use your weight to keep it level fore and aft.

Avoid nose diving....

...or dragging the stern under!

Depending on conditions, the crew and helm usually need to sit close together and avoid depressing the bow or stern too much on all points of sailing. Think of yourself as being part of the boat rather than separate from it — responding to boat balance and trim will soon become something you do without having to think about it.

GYBING. This takes the boat from one tack to the other when sailing downwind by turning the stern of the boat through the wind. To begin, get yourself on a training run, keep the boat flat and raise the centreboard/daggerboard up about three quarters.

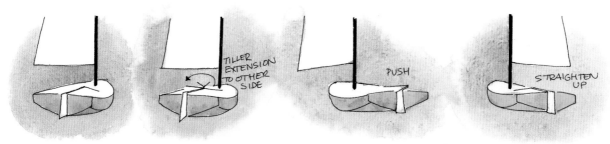

TILLER EXTENSION TO OTHER SIDE

PUSH

STRAIGHTEN UP

Aim to gybe from one training run to another

WIND

WIND

WIND

STAND BY TO GYBE!

GYBE-OH!

WIND ASTERN

As the boom starts to move, helm brings the tiller back to the middle so that helm, boom and tiller are in the middle at the same time. Crew changes jib sheets and moves into the middle of the boat.

Helm sits on new windward side. Crew balances the boat and sets the jib. If centre mainsheet, helm change hands now. (see bit about hand swap under 'tacking')

Check the area is clear – especially under the boom. Helm calls 'stand by to gybe'. Crew also checks area and replies 'yes'. Helm pulls in mainsheet to bring boom clear of the shroud. If aft main, helm changes hands (tiller and mainsheet), moves to middle facing aft, rotating tiller extension to other side. If centre main, face forwards, rotate tiller extension round end of tiller and move into the middle. Call 'Gybe Oh!' and start gybe by pushing tiller to windward – to where you were sitting.

REMEMBER...

CENTRE MAIN... ..face forwards during the gybe and swop hands after the gybe

AFT MAIN... ...change hands before the gybe and face aft during the gybe

Finally.... before moving onto the next chapter, here's an important reminder — it's easy to forget this when you've got so much else to think about!

HOW DO I SLOW DOWN AND STOP?

 35   KEEPING CONTROL

 36   APPROACHING SHORE

38   HOW TO PICK UP A MOORING

Boats don't have brakes! Going fast takes skill, but so does slowing down and stopping because it means being in control at all times. You're safer when you're in control and there won't be so many dents in your hull to patch up at the end of the summer!

KEEPING CONTROL. Most of the time you want your boat to sail as fast as it can go, but unless you know how to slow down and stop, you'll end up damaging your boat - and possibly other people's. You need to slow down if the wind is too strong for you, if you're avoiding collision, sailing into shallow water or coming into shore, or you may just need to pause to sort yourself out.

SLOWING DOWN....

① Reef the sail. Reefing makes the sail area smaller so you can keep control in stronger winds. Reefing is best done before you set off — you can always take the reef out later if the wind eases.

single-handed dinghies often reef by wrapping the sail round the mast

There are many ways of reefing, so find out how it's done on the boat you're sailing.

SLOWING DOWN.... ② Ease sheets

If your sails are not trimmed properly, you'll go slower.

So let the sails out until they flutter....

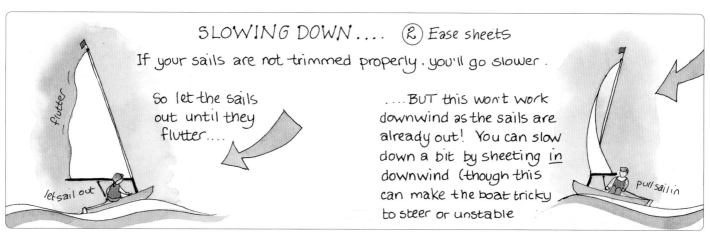

flutter

let sail out

....BUT this won't work downwind as the sails are already out! You can slow down a bit by sheeting in downwind (though this can make the boat tricky to steer or unstable

pull sail in

STOPPING.... if you turn into the wind, the boat will stop - but not for long. Here are two ways to stop and stay in control....

WORKS WITH ONE SAIL OR TWO

① Lying-to

KEEP A GOOD ALL-ROUND LOOKOUT WHEN YOU'RE STOPPED! AND REMEMBER YOU'LL STILL DRIFT DOWNWIND...

② Hove-to

NEEDS TWO SAILS TO MAKE IT WORK

backing the jib means sheeting it in on the windward side

Turn the boat onto a close reach and let the sails out until they flap. To get going again, just sheet in - easy!

This is useful if you want to stop for longer, say, to reef your sail. Turn onto a close reach, let the sails out, then back the jib and push the tiller over to leeward.

APPROACHING SHORE. Whether it's a slipway, beach, pontoon or mooring, you need to know how to slow down and stop in a controlled way. On a beach or slipway you can't choose the wind direction for your approach, but on a pontoon or mooring you usually can. Plan ahead and think it through before you get too close!

When you sail in tidal waters you need to take tides into account when coming onto a pontoon or picking up a mooring. Chapter Seven looks at tides in more detail, so for now we'll just think about ...

Have you noticed boats have no brakes?

CATCH ME, MUM!

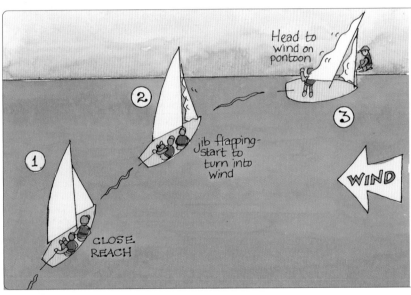

ONTO A PONTOON ......

① Approach on a close reach, controlling your speed by pulling in or letting out your sails.

② Your boat will carry on moving even after your sails start flapping so don't approach too quickly!

③ Stop in the lying-to position and use your painter to tie on to the pontoon.

... ONTO A BEACH OR SLIPWAY ...

Use the same method as above, but remember to raise the centreboard/daggerboard as you get shallower!

THERE YOU GO, MUM — YOU WON'T EVEN GET YOUR FEET WET!

How do I slow down and stop?

WITH AN ONSHORE WIND. Sometimes you need to stop downwind, which is quite easy in a boat with two sails.

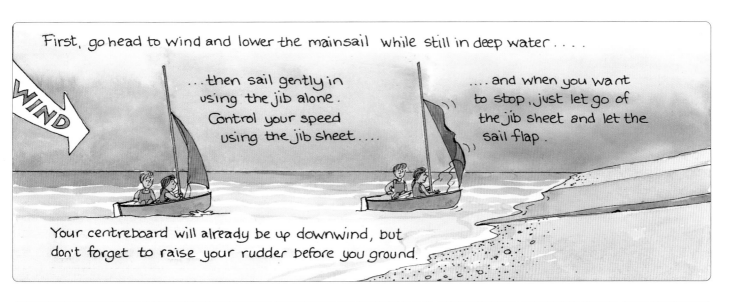

First, go head to wind and lower the mainsail while still in deep water . . . .

...then sail gently in using the jib alone. Control your speed using the jib sheet . . . .

. . . and when you want to stop, just let go of the jib sheet and let the sail flap.

WIND

Your centreboard will already be up downwind, but don't forget to raise your rudder before you ground.

If you've only got one sail and it's hoisted with a halyard . . . .

. . . . turn head to wind and lower the sail most of the way.

Make sure you don't get tangled up in the sail as you lower it!

boats with a gaff can lower this to slow down

make sure you leave enough sail up to keep moving

WIND

Remember to raise your rudder and centreboard or daggerboard!

WIND

WIND

Coming onto a beach downwind you can turn into wind at the last minute and step over the side.

If the wind is blowing sideways ALONG the beach you can do the same thing — come in on a reach and turn into wind in shallow water.

Chapter Four

HOW TO PICK UP A MOORING. Coming to a stop to pick up a mooring buoy takes practice. To begin with, you'll overshoot or stop too short (usually where lots of people are watching) but it's very satisfying when you get it spot on (this of course will happen when no-one is watching!)

Approach the buoy on a close reach so that you can control your speed with the sails.....

Stop in the lying-to position with the buoy by your windward shroud so that the crew can reach it and tie on to it.

If you're single-handed, use the same approach.....

... and stop with the buoy as far forward as you can reach.

Stopped too soon? Sail away and try again!

Too fast, sailed straight past ....
.... don't take risks, sail round for another go.

Picking up a buoy can be a useful way to take a break ...

When you've got hold of the buoy there's usually a length of rope under it to tie to the boat. (Read about knots in Chapter Seven)

YUM! YUM!

This line is attached to a heavier line or chain connected to a heavy weight on the sea bed - you hope!

HOW DO I CHOOSE A BOAT?

41 HOW MUCH WILL IT COST?

42 WHERE CAN I KEEP HER?

43 WHAT TYPE DO I CHOOSE?

46 WHERE DO I LAUNCH?

Choosing a boat is like choosing a friend. You need to get on well and enjoy the same things. There are hundreds of boats out there – how do you choose the right one for you?

How do I choose a boat?

HOW MUCH WILL IT COST? Now you've learnt the basics, you're ready for a boat of your own. What do you choose and how much will it cost? Serious racing will cost serious money, but for most of us, getting afloat needn't cost a fortune.

Boats used to be made out of wood or plywood – some still are, but most are now made of grp (fibreglass) or moulded plastic. Modern materials are more expensive to buy but take less looking after than wood.

BUYING NEW

Boat shows and dinghy shows are a good place to start as they have all the latest designs as well as up to date versions of popular classes. Shows are useful for research if you want to window-shop before buying secondhand .....

SHOW OFFER £3,500

COME ON, DAD!

BUYING SECONDHAND

Sailing club noticeboards, small ads in sailing magazines and the internet are all good places to look (most dinghy class associations have a website). Dinghies have a long life if they're looked after so you can pick up an older boat for a few hundred pounds.

Take someone experienced with you when you look at a boat for sale – one that looks like a bargain might need a lot of money spent on it.

...A BIT OF FILLER AND A LICK OF PAINT, SHE'LL BE GOOD AS NEW!

DON'T FORGET ABOUT INSURANCE!

You'll need dinghy insurance in case of accidents or damage – not just to your own boat but other people's! It's not expensive and sailing clubs may ask to see proof of insurance before you can race.

GLUG GLUG

...CREDIT CARD NUMBER IS.....

WHERE CAN I KEEP HER? When you buy a boat, ask if it comes with a trailer. Most dinghies will have a launching trolley to get them into the water but if you want to tow her home you'll need a road trailer too. A combi-trailer combines the two, one on top of the other – they're expensive but make transport and launching very easy. Make sure you buy the right trailer for the size of boat.

Small dinghies like toppers, optimists and mirrors, can go on the roof of the car, but most need a road trailer unless you live round the corner from your sailing club!

If you join a sailing club, there will be a dinghy park to keep your boat, although you may have to bring her home for the winter. If you don't have space in a garden or garage, find a friend who does!

A larger dinghy can be kept on a mooring, which saves time launching and rigging every time you sail. But you'll need to paint her bottom with special paint called antifoul to keep weed off, and a cover is useful to keep the rain out.

You'll also need to keep a small dinghy on shore to row out to her!

How do I choose a boat?

WHAT TYPE DO I CHOOSE? For a start, decide if you want to race. If you do, even at a simple level, it's a good idea to choose a well known class of dinghy so you can race with others on equal terms (it also means your boat will be easy to sell). See what's popular at your sailing club. There is so much choice of boat it can get very confusing, so here are just a few of the most popular types..... starting with the smallest!

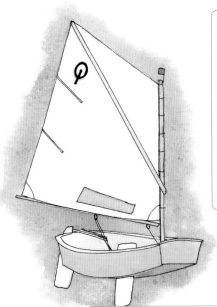

OPTIMIST – Children have learnt to sail in 'oppies' for 50 years and they are still popular. There is an active racing circuit. Made from wood or grp.

LASER FUNBOAT – Very simple beginner dinghy, twin hulled with no centreboard so easy to launch off the beach.

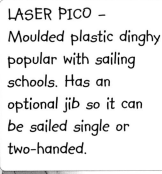

TOPPER – Simple and robust plastic dinghy for children and lightweight adults. Easy to transport and launch. A junior class racing dinghy up to age 16.

LASER PICO – Moulded plastic dinghy popular with sailing schools. Has an optional jib so it can be sailed single or two-handed.

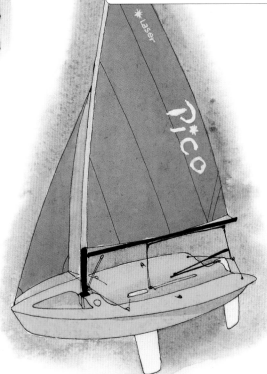

MIRROR – Popular since the 1960s, made of plywood or grp. A junior class racing boat, but also great for taking mum and dad for a cruise!

LASER 4.7 Idea for younger sailors, the 4.7 is the smallest of 3 rigs that fit the standard laser hull, so very adaptable. A youth and Olympic class dinghy raced with the larger radial or full size rigs.

CADET – Designed for two children to sail. Now made of grp but plenty of secondhand plywood cadets available. An active National racing circuit.

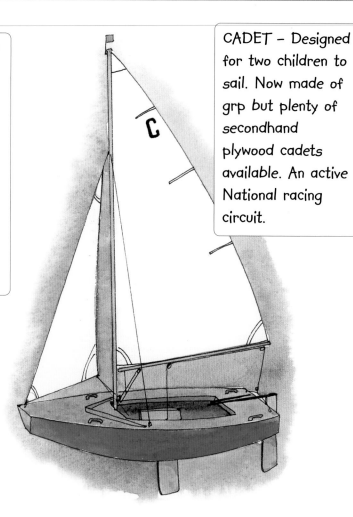

RS FEVA – A modern moulded plastic dinghy for older children and adults. The Feva XL has a more powerful rig.

29ER A fast and exciting National youth racing dinghy – not for beginners!

If there's more than two of you, you'll need something bigger and more stable. If you don't want to race, you can be more individual in your choice......

WAYFARER – A versatile and roomy dinghy for racing or cruising. Originally made from wood but now in grp. Capable of longer coastal cruises.

DART 16 This is a catamaran with two hulls and no centreboard. Catamarans are fast – the Dart is one type easy for beginners to sail.

DEVON LUGGER This is about as big as a dinghy gets! Stable and spacious, boats like Drascombes and Devons can carry the whole family and plenty of gear – popular with sea schools and youth groups as there's room for instructor and several students.

DON'T BE LEFT OUT IF YOU'RE DISABLED !
There are plenty of boats you can sail – try bigger dinghies like the lugger or, if you want to go for speed, try the specially adapted Challenger trimaran.
RYA SAILABILITY will give you more details

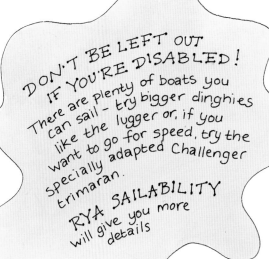

REMEMBER - the faster the boat, the more experience it takes to sail. Don't take on too much too soon, you'll learn more on a boat that doesn't scare you witless!

WHERE DO I LAUNCH? If you join a sailing club you'll have use of a slipway and pontoon as well as a dinghy park. But part of the fun of having a small boat is sailing somewhere new – there are hundreds of places to launch on the coast, up estuaries and on inland waters. If you're on holiday you can sometimes get temporary membership of a club and use their facilities.

SAILING CENTRES

Most inland lakes and waterways need a permit before you can launch. The most popular areas have sailing centres where you can launch, leave your trailer, and pay for as long as you need.

Some, like Rutland Water, provide rescue cover too.

QUACK!

PUBLIC SLIPWAYS

Many harbours have a public slipway for anyone to use – you may have to pay a small fee. If there isn't a public slipway then a marina or boatyard may have one.

There may not be much room to leave cars and trailers at a public slip - the harbour office will advise. A useful book is 'Where to Launch around the Coast' available from chandlers. There are also websites.

Public slipways get very busy in summer!

OFF THE BEACH

Make sure you have firm level sand or shingle. Surf, rocks or soft mud are bad news!

HOW DO I STAY SAFE ?

49 AVOID THAT SINKING FEELING

50 HOW TO AVOID COLLISIONS

52 WHAT IF I CAPSIZE?

53 HOW TO MAKE A TOW

54 MAN OVERBOARD!

55 WHAT IF THE WIND DROPS?

56 INDEPENDENT SAILING

56 HOW TO CALL FOR HELP

Sailing is always an adventure, and as in all adventures you need to be well prepared to stay safe. Treat the water with respect - it's real, not a computer game!

AVOID THAT SINKING FEELING! Dinghies need to be unsinkable so that they stay afloat even when capsized. Many modern boats have watertight compartments built in but others may have blow up buoyancy bags strapped in. Check that the buoyancy in your boat is adequate and not going to leak or fall out if the boat capsizes.

Dinghies are weight sensitive! Don't overload your boat with more than it's designed for.

I THINK YOU'VE PUT A BIT TOO MUCH AIR IN....

YOU PUMP, I'LL BAIL!

Boats with an open stern like this are self draining to let the water out. If your boat doesn't have a self-draining cockpit you'll need a bailer to scoop the water out. Make sure your bailer is tied onto the boat!

Chapter Six

HOW TO AVOID COLLISIONS? Popular sailing areas get very busy and you need to make sure you don't hit anything! There is a highway code for the water just like on land - it's called the International Regulations for Prevention of Collision at Sea and you need to know the basics to avoid dangerous and expensive crashes. Remember, boats don't have brakes.

PORT TACK GIVES WAY TO STARBOARD

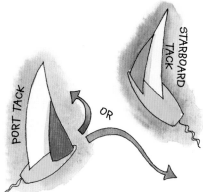

A boat on port tack must keep clear of a boat on starboard tack.

If you're on starboard, hold your course but stay on guard in case the port tack boat hasn't seen you.

If you're not sure which tack a boat is on - for example if it's flying a spinnaker and you can't see the mainsail, assume it's on starboard and keep clear.

WINDWARD BOAT KEEPS CLEAR

If two boats are on the same tack, the windward boat has to keep clear.

If you're sailing in a very busy area, it's important to control your speed - the faster you're moving, the more damage you'll do if you hit something. Get used to knowing which tack you're on at all times, so that you don't have to work it out when deciding whether to alter course.

DON'T PANIC, IT'S FINE - WE'RE ON STARBOARD TACK!

MENACE

POWER GIVES WAY TO SAIL

... but there are exceptions!

Use your common sense and if in doubt, keep out of the way.

brm, brm...

Remember, you are under power if you are rowing or paddling.

DRIVE ON THE RIGHT

On a river or narrow channel stay on the right hand side if you can, whether under power or sail.

OVERTAKING BOAT KEEPS CLEAR

chug chug

When overtaking another boat, keep out of its way - even if you're a sailing boat overtaking a power boat!

LOOKOUT!

'EVERY VESSEL SHALL AT ALL TIMES MAINTAIN A PROPER LOOKOUT'

This is the most important rule, and it sounds easy, but remember to keep an all-round watch. On sailing boats there is usually a blind spot behind the jib that you need to be aware of.

At sea, everyone has an equal responsibility to avoid collision. If someone doesn't give way for you when they should, then it's up to you to move out of the way!

WHAT IF I CAPSIZE? Dinghies do capsize occasionally - but it's nothing to worry about if you're prepared and know what to do. When you start sailing you'll learn to capsize and right your boat in a safe situation so that it won't be a shock when it happens for real.

DON'T PANIC! Your buoyancy aid will help keep you afloat so save your energy for pulling the boat upright.

STAY WITH THE BOAT

WAIT FOR ME!

This is important as your boat may blow downwind faster than you can swim.

RIGHTING A TWO PERSON BOAT .....

1. Helm and crew swim to the stern and hold on. Check the rudder is still on.

2. Helm takes the end of the mainsheet and swims round to the centreboard.

3. Once there, helm stabilises the boat so it doesn't invert (turn upside-down).

4. Crew finds the jib sheet and passes it to helm.

5. Helm can then let go of the mainsheet and climb onto the centreboard holding the jib sheet.

6. Crew floats inside the boat holding on to a toe strap.

DON'T PANIC! If you find yourself in the water under the sail, put your hand up to create a space and then swim to the side

upper jib sheet

7. Helm stands with feet close to hull and leans back on the jib sheet.

8. As the boat comes upright the crew is scooped back on board. Crew can then help helm back on board.

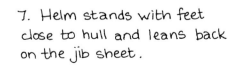

RIGHTING A SINGLEHANDED DINGHY

1. Swim to the stern and check the rudder.

2. Hold the mainsheet and swim to the daggerboard.

3. To right the boat, pull on the daggerboard or climb onto it.

4. As you pull on the side of the hull, the boat will right itself and you can climb back in.

Make sure the mast is pointing downwind as you right the boat. Otherwise the sail will fill and the boat might flip over on the other side!

DON'T GET TOO COLD

Capsizing can leave you cold and wet — if you start shivering, go ashore to get warm and dry.

HOW TO TAKE A TOW

Pass your painter to the rescue boat, lower your sail & raise the centreboard. Leave the rudder in so you can steer. Sit near the back of the boat so the bow stays high.

FASTER, FASTER!

If several boats are being towed one behind the other, the last boat keeps his rudder in to steer.

Chapter Six

MAN OVERBOARD! Falling overboard from a dinghy doesn't happen very often but if it does, you need to know what to do....

If you're helming and your crew falls overboard, let the jib sheet go immediately. If you are the crew and your helm falls out, release the jib sheet and grab the tiller to regain control of the boat.

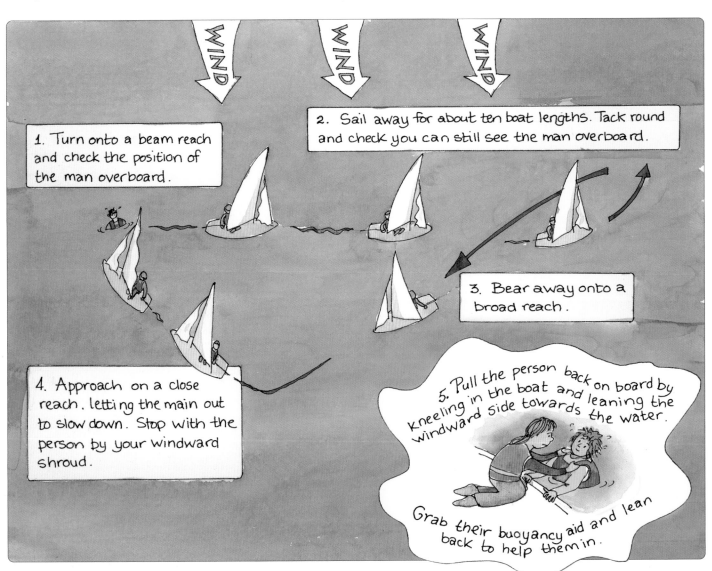

WHAT IF THE WIND DROPS? If there's no wind at all, or you can't sail because you've broken some gear, you need to be able to paddle or row to safety if you can. Make sure you carry oars or a paddle and know how to use them. Rowing is like riding a bicycle – tricky to start with but once it's clicked you never lose it....

ROWING

Practise in calm conditions close to shore. The secret is to move both hands together in small circles, pulling at the top of each stroke as the oar blade goes through the water.

Try to get into a rhythm – if you get in a muddle, stop and start again. Row against the tide or wind if you can, so if you get tired it will carry you home.

Don't dig the blades in too deep - just below the surface is best

SMALL CIRCLES HERE ....

.... MAKE BIG CIRCLES HERE

To turn right, use the left oar only and vice versa.
To stop, dig both blades into the water and hold it.

PADDLING

This is easier if there are two of you - one to paddle and one to steer. Sit as far forward as possible to paddle.

If you're single-handed, sit on the tiller extension to steer or use a one-handed paddle!

HINT –
If you have to row or paddle against a strong tide or river current, stay as close to the bank as you can where the flow will be weakest.

Chapter Six

INDEPENDENT SAILING – if you want to sail without rescue cover, you'll need to be well equipped and prepared.

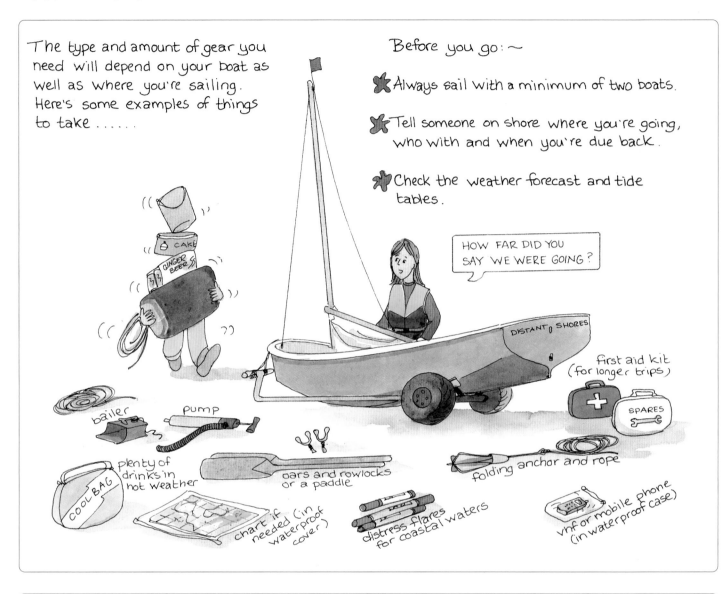

The type and amount of gear you need will depend on your boat as well as where you're sailing. Here's some examples of things to take ......

Before you go :~

🌟 Always sail with a minimum of two boats.

🌟 Tell someone on shore where you're going, who with and when you're due back.

🌟 Check the weather forecast and tide tables.

HOW FAR DID YOU SAY WE WERE GOING?

DISTANT SHORES

first aid kit (for longer trips)

SPARES

bailer

pump

plenty of drinks in hot weather

COOL BAG

oars and rowlocks or a paddle

folding anchor and rope

chart if needed (in waterproof cover)

distress flares for coastal waters

vhf or mobile phone (in waterproof case)

HOW TO CALL FOR HELP....

If you're in difficulty and can't get out by yourself, ask for help. Here's how :~

🌟 Use a mobile phone or vhf.

🌟 Shout, wave something or blow a whistle.

🌟 Move your arms steadily up and down like this .....

🌟 In coastal waters, use distress flares. Make sure you read the instructions and know how to use them.

distress flares?

WHAT ELSE DO I NEED TO KNOW?

59   WEATHER BASICS

60   WHAT ABOUT WIND DIRECTION?

61   HOW DO WE MEASURE WIND STRENGTH?

62   WHAT ABOUT TIDES?

63   TIDAL FLOW

64   HOW DO YOU STOP IN TIDAL WATERS?

66   GET KNOTTED!

67   LOOK AFTER YOUR BOAT....

There's more to sailing than sailing!

Seamanship is all about an awareness of your surroundings, understanding wind and tide, and getting to know your boat so well that you work as a team. So stay alert, ask questions, spend as much time on the water as you can and you'll soon become a wise old salt!

WEATHER BASICS.....

You don't need to be a meteorologist (try saying that with a mouth full of toffee....) but you need to know what the wind is going to do before you sail – and if it's going to change in strength or direction while you're out sailing. You can get a forecast from club/harbour noticeboards, internet, ceefax, radio, tv and phone - the internet is one of the most accurate as it is updated regularly. If you are sailing on coastal waters, the best bet is the inshore waters forecast from the Met Office.

WHAT DO THE WORDS IN THE FORECAST MEAN? You don't need to know them all but they're all very exact. Here are a few useful ones ...

IMMINENT — means within six hours
SOON — means six to twelve hours
LATER — means after twelve hours

CAPTAIN SCURVY'S SHIPPING FORECAST FOR LAZY SAILORS...

... if a candle stays alight outdoors, there's not enough wind to sail. If it blows out, there's too much!

WEATHER FORECASTS MADE SIMPLE...
Two types of weather systems determine our weather, high pressure and low pressure.

HIGH PRESSURE
- settled weather, dry with light winds

LOW PRESSURE
unsettled weather, wet and windy

Chapter Seven

WHAT ABOUT WIND DIRECTION? The forecast will give you wind direction - remember it describes where the wind is coming from not blowing to. Get to know the points of the compass in your sailing area so that you know what to expect.

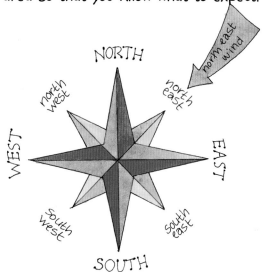

LOCAL EFFECTS - get to know your sailing area. River valleys can funnel wind, trees and hills can make it tricky, and it is usually windier off headlands than in bays.

plenty of wind here

not much wind here

WIND DIRECTION IS ESPECIALLY IMPORTANT ON THE COAST....

Breaking waves can make launching and recovery tricky...

WATCH OUT !

.... but it will be downwind sailing home

ONSHORE WIND

OFFSHORE WIND

..... but waves will be bigger offshore - if you get into difficulties you'll be blown further out to sea.

WATCH OUT !

Nice and easy to launch and recover ......

HOW SEA BREEZES WORK...

Sea breezes happen in spring and summer when the land heats up quicker than the sea.....

HOT SUN

land heats up and hot air rises...

... air cools and falls

...air is drawn on shore

SEA BREEZE

LAND

SEA

CROSS-SHORE WIND

Easy to launch and recover and a beam reach to and from shore. Perfect! The windward end of the beach may be more sheltered than the downwind end.

HOW DO WE MEASURE WIND STRENGTH?

In the 18th century Admiral Beaufort made up the Beaufort Scale to help sailors work out wind strength. It was based on describing the sea state in different winds and goes from Force 0 to Force 12. It is still the system we use today.

Force 12.... Hurricane... .... Admirals blown over......

WHEN IS A KNOT NOT A KNOT?

When it's a nautical mile per hour, used to measure wind speed (and boat speed). A nautical mile is a bit longer than a land mile.

NOT A KNOT

KNOT

BEAUFORT SCALE FOR BEGINNERS

FORCE 0 calm

No wind at all - but look out for ripples on the water that tell you wind is coming.

FORCE 2 light breeze

4-6 knots of wind. So nice and gentle you could take your granny out!

FORCE 1 light air

1-3 knots of wind. You can sail, but only just. A bit frustrating.

FORCE 4 moderate breeze
11-15 knots of wind. Time for beginners to head for home and watch the experts from ashore!

FORCE 3 gentle breeze

7-10 knots of wind. Perfect sailing!

FORCE 5 and above? Don't even think about it! Experienced sailors can cope up to Force 6 but by Force 7 everyone is in the clubhouse!

WHAT ABOUT TIDES? If you only sail on a lake, you can skip the next four pages, but if you plan to sail on the coast, estuaries and rivers, you need to know how tides work and how they will affect you. Tides come in (flood) and go out (ebb) twice in every 24 hours.

WHAT CAUSES TIDES?
Tides are caused by the gravitational pull of the sun and moon. There are two spring tides and two neap tides every month, which is the time it takes the moon to go round the earth.

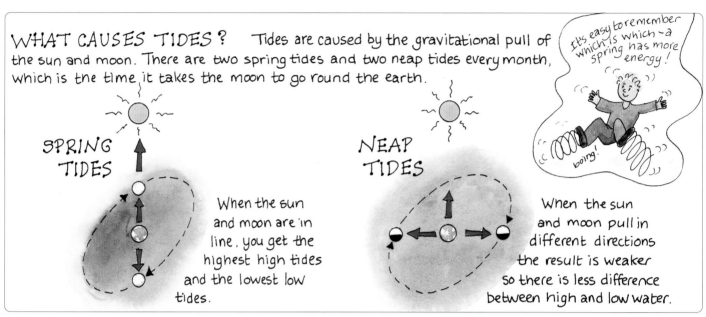

SPRING TIDES
When the sun and moon are in line, you get the highest high tides and the lowest low tides.

NEAP TIDES
When the sun and moon pull in different directions the result is weaker so there is less difference between high and low water.

It's easy to remember which is which — a spring has more energy!

boing!

TIDAL RANGE
The difference in height between high and low tide is called the range. If you sail in a place with a big tidal range, get to know it at low tide!

high water springs
high water neaps

low water neaps
low water springs

WELL, IT WASN'T HERE WHEN WE CAME OUT!

JUNE	TIME (GMT)	HEIGHT OF TIDE (metres)	
15 SA	0120	4.3	← HIGH
	0737	0.6	← LOW
	1344	4.6	← HIGH
	2011	0.8	← LOW

There are two high tides and two low tides every day, so there is just over six hours between each high and low. Remember to add an hour for BST in summer.

PLAN AHEAD!

NO, YOU GET OUT & PUSH!

If you want to explore tidal creeks, go up on a rising tide and then head for home before it drops too far! You can find out the times of high and low water using tide tables like this.

TIDAL FLOW. The tide takes approximately six hours to flood and six hours to ebb, with a small time in between called slack water when the tide is changing direction. It is important to know which way the tide is going and when it is going to change direction as it will affect your sailing....

CATCH A RIDE ON A TIDE!
If you have a choice, sail home with the tide. The wind might disappear but the tides are always reliable!

THERE'S SOMETHING FISHY GOING ON...

GO WITH THE FLOW — TRAVEL QUICKLY

How do you tell which way the tide is flowing?

Look at how it flows round a fixed object.

GO AGAINST THE FLOW — CAN BE SLOW

Wind opposite tide... ...makes a bumpy ride

WIND

TIDE

Wind and tide together mean flat water... it can be windier than it looks!

WIND

TIDE

WATCH OUT!

Don't forget about tides when you go ashore! If you're coming ashore onto a beach or slipway, pull your boat up the beach if the tide is rising.

TIDE? WHAT TIDE?

LOTS OF WIND

plus...

LITTLE TIDE

= NO PROBLEM

LITTLE WIND

plus...

BIG TIDE

= PROBLEM!

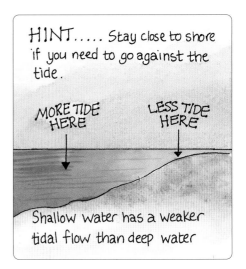

HINT..... Stay close to shore if you need to go against the tide.

MORE TIDE HERE

LESS TIDE HERE

Shallow water has a weaker tidal flow than deep water

TIDES CAN ALSO PUSH YOU SIDEWAYS......

Tides aren't always with or against you - sometimes you'll be sailing across the tidal flow. So it's no good pointing your boat in the direction you want to go if the water you're sailing on is moving sideways! Head uptide of your destination -

lining up two objects on shore can help you keep on track. The stronger the tide, the more allowance you'll need to make.

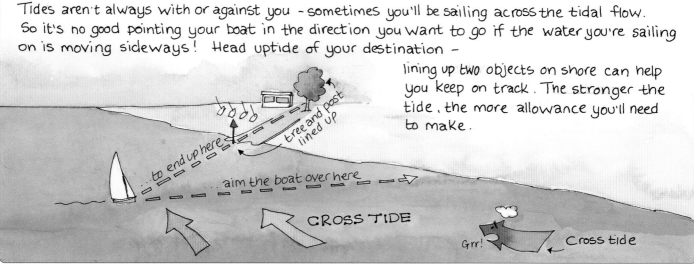

... to end up here
tree and post lined up
...aim the boat over here
CROSS TIDE
Grr!
Cross tide

HOW DO YOU STOP IN TIDAL WATERS? Tides also make a difference when you're trying to pick up a mooring. The trickiest combination of wind and tide is when they are opposite each other - trying to use the wind as your brake won't work if there's a strong tide under you! Here's what to do about picking up and setting off from a mooring.....

PICKING UP A MOORING....

When wind and tide are opposite, approaching into wind won't work. Use the tide as your brake and approach downwind.

WIND

Turn head to wind first to drop the mainsail, then approach the buoy downwind using the jib sheet to control your speed.

Let the jib fly while you pick up the buoy and secure the boat.

TIDE

LEAVING A MOORING.....

Have you noticed boats on a mooring lie downtide? When wind and tide are opposite, you can't be head to wind to hoist your mainsail, so hoist your jib instead and sail off the mooring downwind.

WIND

Make sure your mainsail is prepared ready to hoist before you sail off.

When you've got a clear space, turn into wind and hoist the main.

TIDE

Wind and tide in opposite directions also makes a difference when approaching and leaving a pontoon......

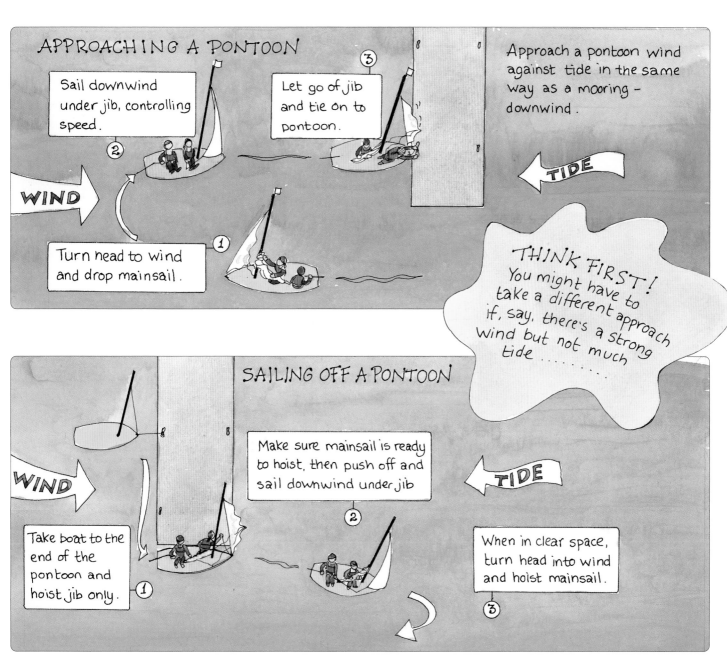

APPROACHING A PONTOON

Sail downwind under jib, controlling speed.

②

Let go of jib and tie on to pontoon.

③

Turn head to wind and drop mainsail.

①

WIND

TIDE

Approach a pontoon wind against tide in the same way as a mooring – downwind.

THINK FIRST!
You might have to take a different approach if, say, there's a strong wind but not much tide . . . .

SAILING OFF A PONTOON

WIND

Take boat to the end of the pontoon and hoist jib only.

①

Make sure mainsail is ready to hoist, then push off and sail downwind under jib

②

TIDE

When in clear space, turn head into wind and hoist mainsail.

③

I'M A BIT TIDE UP AT THE MOMENT...

With practice you'll get used to working out what the tide is doing to you - remember the tide can be a good friend but a bad enemy !

That's enough about tides for now - let's take a look at getting all 'tied up' in a very different way.....

GET KNOTTED! All sailors need to know how to tie knots, but you also need to learn which knot to use for which job. These are the most useful, so keep a piece of spare rope in your pocket and practise these for starters......

What Knot?	What's it for?	How do I tie it?
REEF KNOT	Tying a rope round something, or tying two ropes together (as long as they're the same thickness) Traditionally used for tying reef points in a sail.	Easy - you probably know this one ... ...and under right over left... left over right... ...and under
FIGURE OF EIGHT	A stopper knot tied at the end of a rope to stop it slipping through a block.	Easy - make the shape of an '8' on its side and you're nearly there ..... ① make a loop ... ② pass under the line.. ③ .. then bring the end back through the loop
ROUND TURN & TWO HALF HITCHES	Tying a rope to a post or ring, often used for tying mooring lines.	① loop over the post ② bring the end round into a half hitch ... ③ ...then do another half-hitch and pull tight
BOWLINE pronounced "BOW-LIN"	For making a secure loop in a rope, used for attaching sheets to the corner of a sail.	Tricky to start with but stick with it and practise until you can do it without thinking.

① 'STANDING PART' = the longest bit
make a small twist like this and hold it at the crossover. Make sure the 'standing part' is at the back

② bring the free end through the loop...
leave a nice big loop here

③ carry on behind the standing part, back into the loop and down.
Pull tight!
this bit should always end up in the middle

Boat maintenance isn't a chore, it's as much a part of good seamanship as trimming sails. This page gives you a few things to do regularly during the season, and the next page tells you what to do at the beginning and end of each sailing year. Different types of boat need looking after in different ways, but these are a few basics....

LOOK AFTER YOUR BOAT.... and your boat will look after you!

LOW MAINTENANCE DOESN'T MEAN NO MAINTENANCE......

Even the most robust grp or plastic dinghy will suffer wear and tear when exposed to salt water, sand, mud and shingle. Try to keep her looking good.

gleam gleam

Keep your boat hosed down with fresh water if you sail in salt water. Pay attention to the centreboard casing which can fill with mud and shingle if the boat is dragged up the beach.

PING!

keep an eye on all your fittings - worn toe-straps can lead to a dunking!

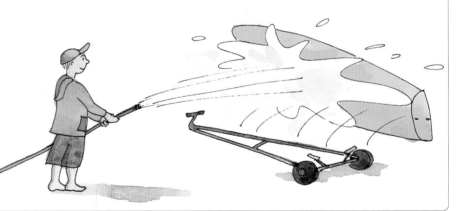

I THINK IT'S SAFE TO SAY WE'VE WON THIS ONE, CHARLIE!

Ropes wear out and chafe in places so check them regularly, along with shackles, blocks and rudder fittings.

AT THE END OF THE SEASON ......

When it's time to pack up for the winter, take all the gear off the boat and take it home. It's a good idea to label your ropes, shackles and blocks before you put them away!

If you have a boat cover, use it. If not, turn her upside down on the trailer so the cockpit doesn't fill with dead leaves and gunge.

Wash your sails in warm soapy water in the bath if you're allowed to....

..... and the ropes can be washed gently in the washing machine — take all the blocks and shackles off first!

Store everything in a dry airy place for the winter.

AT THE BEGINNING OF THE SEASON ......

If you labelled all your rigging, you won't have problems remembering where everything goes! Check all gear for wear and tear as you put it back together again.

Check your boat carefully. Make sure deck fittings aren't starting to pull away from the deck.

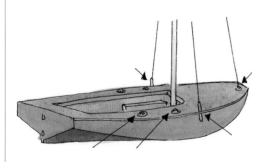

If your boat is wood she'll need rubbing down with sandpaper, then painting and/or varnishing. This is not just to make her look good - bare wood will rot when wet so it's to keep her protected and shipshape. Don't think of it as a chore - use the time to plan those sunny days afloat!

WHAT NEXT

71   SAILING FASTER

72   START RACING!

74   LETS GO EXPLORING!

76   GO SAILING!

You never stop learning every time you sail, but as you gain experience you'll want to expand your horizons. Do you want to go faster? Go further? Or both? This chapter gives a few suggestions about how to develop your sailing skills.

What next?

SAILING FASTER. To go faster off the wind you can set a big sail called a spinnaker. Conventional spinnakers are quite complicated to handle, but an asymmetric spinnaker is easier as it is simply a big reaching jib designed to catch bucket loads of wind! It's used between a beam reach and a broad reach and decreases in power the further away from the wind you steer. The zone diagram shows you where to hoist, power up, depower and drop the sail in relation to the wind.

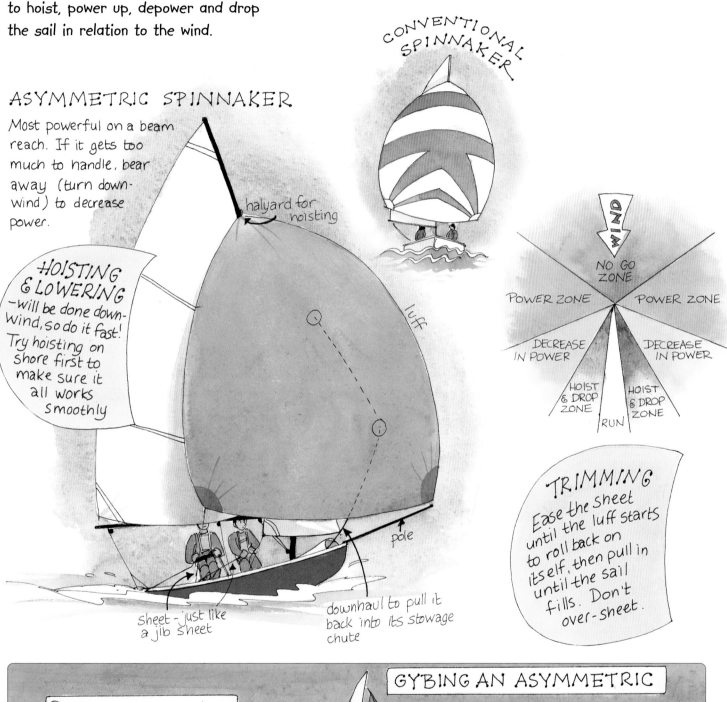

CONVENTIONAL SPINNAKER

ASYMMETRIC SPINNAKER

Most powerful on a beam reach. If it gets too much to handle, bear away (turn down-wind) to decrease power.

halyard for hoisting

HOISTING & LOWERING -will be done down-wind, so do it fast! Try hoisting on shore first to make sure it all works smoothly

luff

pole

sheet - just like a jib sheet

downhaul to pull it back into its stowage chute

WIND
NO GO ZONE
POWER ZONE   POWER ZONE
DECREASE IN POWER   DECREASE IN POWER
HOIST & DROP ZONE   HOIST & DROP ZONE
RUN

TRIMMING Ease the sheet until the luff starts to roll back on itself, then pull in until the sail fills. Don't over-sheet.

GYBING AN ASYMMETRIC

① Steer a gentle curve into the gybe. Crew takes up slack on leeward sheet.

WIND

② 'Gybe-oh!' Moving across the boat, crew keeps the original sheet tight while the sail flattens against the jib, then sheets in on the other side as it comes across.

③ Trim sheets, balance the boat and off you go!

Chapter Eight

START RACING! You can race dinghies at any level, from fun club races to class racing at national or even international level. If you're not very competitive, use club racing as an opportunity to improve your sailing skills and get the best out of your boat. Start by crewing for someone else so you can learn how it all works.

SAILING INSTRUCTIONS

Study the sailing instructions before you go on the water – they might look complicated but they'll give you details of the course, start times, and where the start and finish lines are. Don't be afraid to ask for help if you don't understand something.

THE COURSE

The course can be any shape and size, but it will be marked with buoys and you'll be told which way round to go, and how many times.

The start line could be the same as the finish line, between a buoy and the committee boat. The committee boat will sound the signals and show the flags for starting and finishing.

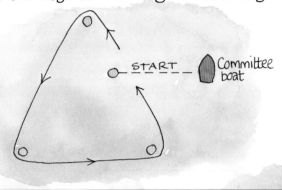

START LINES

The race officer will display flags and make sound signals to count down to the start. The usual sequence is –

.....5 minutes to go

.... 4 minutes to go

.... 1 minute to go

.... GO!

HOW CAN THEY START THE RACE IF THEY WON'T STAY STILL?

The idea is to cross the line going in the right direction as soon after the start as possible. It takes experience to judge where to be and how fast to go to cross the line bang on time.

If you cross the line <u>before</u> the start you will either have to re-cross the start line or be disqualified.

WATCH IT! You'll need a good waterproof watch to help you count down to the start

THE RACING RULES

Just like there are rules for cycling on the road, there are rules on the water for when you go racing. It's designed to be fair and allow everyone a chance to get round the race course. You don't need to learn the racing rules all at once. The basic rules of the road (see Chapter Six) are a good start.

KEEP CLEAR if you are the give way boat, AVOID COLLISIONS, SAIL A PROPER COURSE, and GIVE ROOM (give another boat space to manoeuvre past a mark or obstruction)

IMPROVING YOUR SKILL

If someone is going faster than you in the same type of boat on the course, ask yourself same -why?

Is it sail trim? Centreboard position? Boat trim? Or are they concentrating hard on every wind shift?

THE SOCIAL SCENE

Whether you race at local or national level, there's bound to be a get-together afterwards!

HANDICAP RACING

Handicap racing gives bigger and faster boats a time penalty so that different types of boat can compete on equal terms.

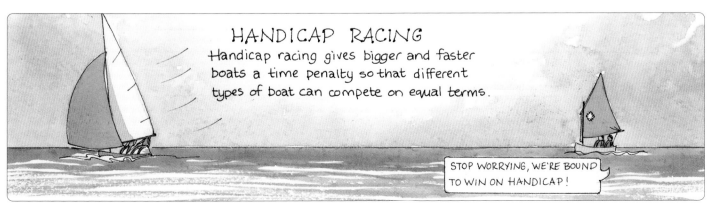

LET'S GO EXPLORING! Sailing is a great way to explore new places but to find out where you can sail, where the hazards are and where you can stop for lunch, you'll need a chart, like this.

MAPS FOR SAILORS - Charts are great because they tell you everything you need to know about the watery bits. Like land maps charts use symbols to show useful and important features on land and sea

Lines of LONGITUDE run from pole to pole like the segments of an orange........

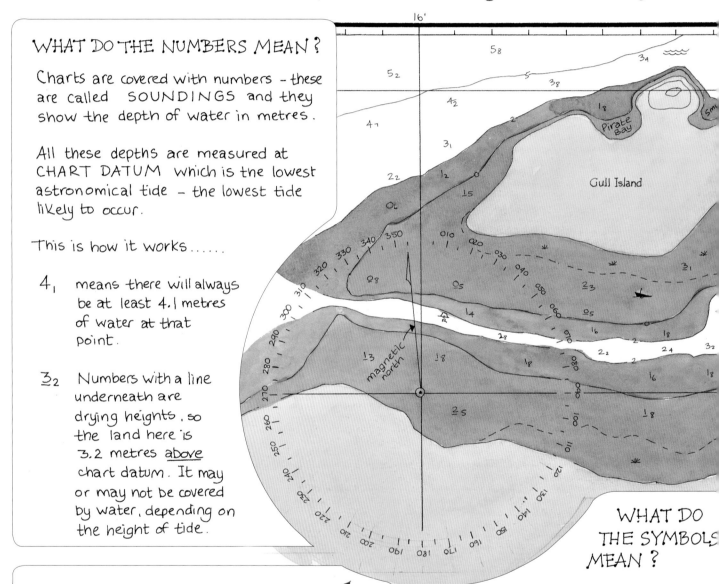

WHAT DO THE NUMBERS MEAN?

Charts are covered with numbers - these are called SOUNDINGS and they show the depth of water in metres.

All these depths are measured at CHART DATUM which is the lowest astronomical tide - the lowest tide likely to occur.

This is how it works......

4_1 means there will always be at least 4.1 metres of water at that point.

$\underline{3}_2$ Numbers with a line underneath are drying heights, so the land here is 3.2 metres above chart datum. It may or may not be covered by water, depending on the height of tide.

WHAT ABOUT THE COMPASS?

The compass on a chart is called a compass rose. It's divided into degrees, like a circle, so north is 0°, east is 90°, south is 180° and west is 270°

When you use a compass on board to check your course, remember that magnetic north is always a few degrees different from true north. The compass rose on the chart shows you what the difference is

WHAT DO THE SYMBOLS MEAN?

‒ ‒ ‒ shallow channel

⚓ recommended anchorage

⚘ ⚘ marsh or swamp

⁓⁓⁓ overfalls or tide rips

▭ public slipway   ⊙ beacon

⛵ wreck   ⌘ church spire

WHAT DO THE COLOURS MEAN? Charts have contour lines to show the shape of the sea bed in the same way that maps show the shape of the land. Different makes of charts use different colours to show the various depths, but on a large scale Admiralty chart the colours will look like this....

Yellow – land   Green – land at low tide, water at high tide (rock, mud or sand)

Blue – 0 and 2 metres of water at low tide   White – more than 2 metres deep at low tide

This is the scale on the top and bottom of the chart, divided into degrees and minutes.

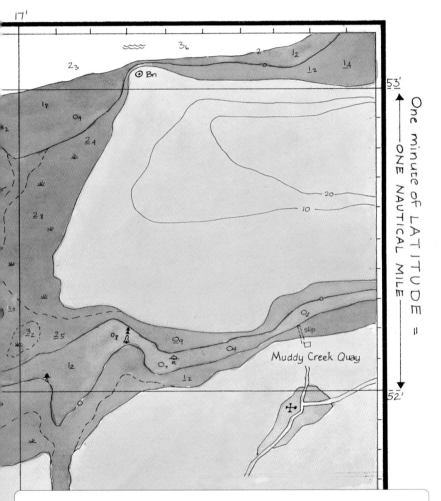

HOW DO I MEASURE DISTANCE?

Distance is measured using lines of LATITUDE – parallel lines running round the world. Each degree of latitude is divided into sixty minutes, and one minute of latitude is a nautical mile.

Confused? Think about the equator, which is 0° – the north pole is 90° N and the south pole is 90° S.

Always use the scale at the side of the chart to measure distance.

Speed is measured in knots – nautical miles per hour.

WHAT ARE THE BUOYS FOR?

Cardinal buoys mark danger points like this.....

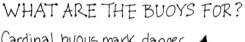

north cardinal

east cardinal

west cardinal

dodgy rock

south cardinal

Cardinal buoys look like this on the chart. The letters BY stand for 'black & yellow'.

Red can buoys mark the port side of a channel when entering harbour.

Green cone buoys mark the starboard side of a channel when entering harbour

GO SAILING! Every time you go out on the water you'll learn something. As your *sea sense* grows, you'll be able to sail better, sail further and sail safely.

A small family cruiser – great for holidays

Sailing a square rigger needn't be just a fantasy – tall ships will take you on board from a young age

The Vendée Globe round the world solo race uses fast boats like this

A modern racing yacht with spinnaker set

A traditional gaff cutter

Whether your dream is to race with the Olympic team, sail round the world or take a picnic up your favourite creek, there's something for everyone. Have a go!

An ocean-going cruiser-racer

small keelboats like this are used for club racing

Ellen MacArthur broke the solo round the world speed record in this fast trimaran

Gaff schooner from the early 20th century – these classic yachts still sail and race today

Luggers like this used to fish for a living, now they sail for fun.

Thames barges used to carry cargo up and down the coast. Now they race and sail for fun

GLOSSARY (what all the words mean)

Aft	at the back of the boat
Astern	behind the boat
Asymmetric	spinnaker flown from retractable pole at bow
Back	'back a jib' means changing tack without changing the jib sheet over, so the sail is the wrong side for the wind
Beam	width of the boat at the widest point or the side of the boat (eg. 'wind on the beam' means the wind is coming sideways on to the boat)
Bear away	turn downwind
Beat	sail a zig zag course to make progress into the wind
Beaufort scale	way of measuring wind strength from force 1 to force 12
Block	a pulley used for hoisting sails etc.
Boom	spar (rigid pole) at the bottom edge of the sail
Bow	front of the boat
Bowline	useful knot with a loop in it
Buoy	floating object attached to the bottom of the sea - some are for navigation, some are for mooring up to, others are temporary to mark out a race course
Buoyancy aid	helps you to stay afloat if you fall in the water
Burgee	small flag at the top of the mast to show wind direction
Catamaran	boat with two hulls
Centreboard	bit that sticks out below the hull to counteract sideways push of the wind and prevent leeway (see also daggerboard). Can be lowered or raised.

Chart datum	depths shown on a chart - at the lowest possible tide
Cleat	device to grip ropes and hold them in place; some grip automatically, others need the rope tying round them
Clew	lower corner of the sail closest to the stern
Close hauled	sailing as near to the wind as you can
Compass rose	the compass shown on a chart to aid navigation
Crew	helps the helmsman to sail the boat, usually handles the jib sheets
Cutter	boat with two headsails (jibs)
Daggerboard	similar function to centreboard, but raised directly up and down rather than on a pivot
Downhaul	puts downward tension on a sail, either a spinnaker or a lug rigged mainsail (also called a Cunningham after its inventor)
Ease	'ease sheets' means letting the sail out gently
Foot	bottom edge of a sail
Fore	towards the front of the boat
Forestay	wire at the front of the boat helping to hold the mast up
Gaff	spar that holds the top edge of a sail extended out from the mast
Gunter	rig that uses a gaff as an extension of the mast (eg. mirror dinghy)
Gunwale	top edge of the hull - the bit you sit on when leaning out to balance the boat

Gybe	to change tack by turning the stern of the boat through the wind
Halyard	rope used to hoist a sail
Head	top corner of a sail
Heave to	stop the boat by easing the main sheet and backing the jib
Heel	a boat 'heels' when it leans over due to the sideways force of the wind
Helm	the person who steers the boat - also the tiller that they steer with
Inversion	a capsize where the boat goes completely upside down (turns turtle)
Jammer	another word for cleat - one that grips the rope and holds it in place until you release it
Jib	smaller sail in front of the mast
Ketch	boat with two masts, a main and mizzen.
Kicking strap (Kicker)	attached to the base of the mast and the boom, helping to hold the boom down
Knot	measurement of speed, based on one minute of latitude
Latitude	imaginary lines running parallel round the globe east-west. They help you to measure position and distance on a chart

Leech	back edge of the sail
Leeward	opposite side to where the wind is blowing
Leeway	the amount of sideways drift caused by the wind
Lie to	a way of stopping the boat temporarily by easing sheets on a close reach
Lifejacket	will keep a person fully afloat with their head clear of the water
Longitude	imaginary lines running round the globe north to south like segments of an orange. Used with lines of latitude to measure position and distance
Luff	front edge of the sail. 'Luffing' means heading the boat directly into the wind
Mast	spar the sails are hoisted up
Meteorology	study of weather forecasting - 'Met Office' is short for 'Meteorological Office'
Mizzen	shorter mast at the back of some boats
Neap Tide	tides with the smallest tidal range
Painter	rope at the bow used to tie the boat to shore
Pontoon	floating jetty to moor your boat to
Port	left had side of the boat (facing forwards)
Reach	sailing with the wind on the side of the boat
Reef	making the sails smaller in strong winds

Rowlocks	U shaped fitting on the gunwales that hold your oars while rowing
Rudder	attached to the stern, controls the direction of the boat
Run	sailing with the wind behind you
Shackle	metal fitting for attaching ropes to blocks etc.
Sheet	rope that controls a sail
Shroud	wires at the side of the mast helping to hold it up
Soundings	numbers on a chart showing depth
Spinnaker	big lightweight sail for faster sailing off the wind
Spring tide	tides with the biggest range and strongest currents
Sprit	spar that runs diagonally across the sail to hold it in place (eg. Optimist rig)
Starboard	right hand side of the boat (facing forwards)
Stern	back of the boat
Tack	a) change direction by turning the bow of the boat through the wind
	b) bottom front corner of a sail
Tidal height	depth of water above chart datum
Tidal range	difference between low and high water
Tidal stream	direction of the tide's flow
Tiller	stick attached to the rudder to steer the boat
Toe straps	straps to tuck your feet under when you lean out to balance the boat

Transit	lining up two fixed objects to keep you on course, for example, if the tide is pushing you sideways
Trim	keeping the boat level fore and aft
Trimaran	boat with three hulls
Wetsuit	neoprene sailing suit to keep you warm when wet
Windward	direction the wind is blowing from
Yawl	boat with a small mizzen mast behind the rudder

Royal Yachting Association   www.rya.org.uk

RYA Sailability (information on sailing for those with disabilities) www.rya.org.uk/sailability

RNLI - for help and advice about safety at sea www.rnli.org.uk

Dinghy Cruising Association www.dca.uk.com

There are lots of websites to look at if you want to buy a dinghy online; here are a few to start with:
www.dinghyshop.co.uk
www.boats-for-sale.co.uk

Dinghy Sailing Magazine
www.seascapemedia.co.uk/dinghysailingmagazine.html
Yachts and Yachting
(in spite of the title has a lot about dinghy sailing and racing!)
www.yachtsandyachting.com

Class Associations/manufacturers - most types of dinghy have a class association and/or website - there is a full list on the RYA website. Here are a few examples:
http://www.rya.org.uk/classes.asp
www.ukmirrorsailing.com
www.optimistsailing.org.uk
www.laser.org.uk
www.gbrtopper.co.uk
www.rs-association.com
www.wayfarer.org.uk
www.29er.org.uk
www.cadetclass.org.uk
www.cometdinghies.com

If you want to find out more about tall ships:

www.asto.org.uk   (has a full list of youth training organisations)

www.tallships.org (has details of Tall Ships Youth Trust)